Capitalism and Class Consciousness
The ideas of Georg Lukács

Chris Nineham

a **COUNTERFIRE** publication

Contents

1. Introduction:
A fight against fatalism

For the last few decades Georg Lukács' work has been kept on the margins of philosophy and socialist theory. As crisis returns to haunt the system it is time for this to change.

Lukács' great achievement, which should by rights ensure him a central place in the radical tradition, was to develop the most coherent account to date of how revolutionary consciousness can emerge under capitalism. To do this, he had to do the opposite; that is, explain how capitalism survives most of the time, despite the misery it creates.

In his key philosophical works of the 1920s, he was fighting against forms of fatalism and passivity that he believed threatened the socialist movement. He was writing at a very different time from our own, but his arguments have an obvious charge now, when the left has the chance to move beyond commentary and start trying to shape reality.

Critics often accuse Lukács the revolutionary of idealism or voluntarism, of believing that the sheer force of ideas could change the world. This is a complete misunderstanding. He was battling to reintegrate human agency into contemporary Marxism, but in a properly dialectical fashion. His crucial breakthrough was to deal convincingly with what appears to be a paradox for revolutionary theory. How can humans be at the centre of the revolutionary process arising out of capitalism, when the great complaint about capitalism is that it makes most of us powerless? How can active human liberation be a product of a dehumanising system?

Another reason his work speaks to us with particular

power today is because it centres on the drastic effects of the capitalist free market on everyday life. Lukács argued that commodification shapes every aspect of our lives. This assessment has been mercilessly borne out by the last thirty years of neoliberal globalisation. But Lukács' analysis allows us to get beyond the two opposing theoretical approaches to commodification which are common on the left. One, characteristic of some of the key intellectual figures of the anti-capitalist movement, is the idea that commodification automatically breeds rebellion. The second is the notion that commodity capitalism degrades the critical faculties of humans beyond repair.

Lukács argued commodification is the secret to both subservience and revolt. Which gains the upper hand depends not on blind forces of history, but on conscious human intervention, and on the way we understand how ideas change.

For all his sometimes dizzying flights of philosophical abstraction, his conclusions are practical. Lukács' achievement in these years was to trace the logic that leads from Marx's *Capital* to Lenin's *What is to be Done?* His arguments help us answer a whole series of immediate questions. In what circumstances does capitalism create resistance? How powerful is ruling class propaganda and how can it be overcome? Where do alternative ideas come from and how can we test their relative value? And last but not least, what can socialists and activists do to accelerate the process of radicalisation?

A philosopher activist

Lukács became a revolutionary and a Marxist during the greatest wave of working class struggle in history, unleashed by the Russian revolution at the end of the First World War. Already a well-known intellectual in Hungary, months after joining the newly-formed Hungarian Communist Party in December 1918 he found himself a leader in the events which led to the brief Hungarian Soviet Republic in

1919. He was People's Commissar for Education and for a short time a political commissar at the battlefront.

The Hungarian Soviet Republic ended in disaster. This was because, as Lukács himself came to recognise, it was unstable from the start. The Hungarian Communist Party had called an insurrection in February 1919 well before it had majority support in the workers' councils. The uprising was crushed, as mass radicalisation proved no substitute for political preparation. All the same, the militancy of peasants and workers and the annexation of parts of the country by foreign powers led to the collapse of the bourgeois government, creating a power vacuum.

The Hungarian Soviet Republic came about in March 1919 through a merger between the Communists and the reformist Social Democratic Party (SDP). The SDP was handed power by the ruling class in a last ditch attempt to salvage the system. Lukács and the leadership of the Communist Party interpreted the new alliance of reformists and revolutionaries as a spontaneous restoration of proletarian unity, but it turned out to be a recipe for confusion and then disaster.

Communist Party leaders acted as if they were in a revolutionary government, forcing through nationalisation of the land with no concern for the interests of the peasantry, while the majority of workers remained under reformist leadership. Faced with new attacks from an alliance of counter-revolutionary powers, the SDP leaders capitulated and the Communists were isolated. A reactionary government was formed, and unleashed a reign of terror on the left, executing 5,000 and driving tens of thousands more out of the country.

Lukács wrote his key works of the 1920s – *Lenin: A Study in the Unity of his Thought, History and Class Consciousness* and *Tailism and the Dialectic* – in the aftermath of this experience, while he was in exile in Vienna. We can see now this was a decisive moment for the socialist movement. Before the war, the world socialist movement had been organised in the Second International. Its complete accommodation to the system was exposed by its leading parties' support for the First World War. The Russian Bolsheviks stood out against this betrayal and led a successful revolution that became an inspiration for millions around the world.

Both *History and Class Consciousness* and *Lenin: A Study in the Unity of his Thought* express the revolutionary potential of the moment, and the fear that lessons were not being learnt from the experience. By 1925, when Lukács wrote *Tailism and the Dialectic*, there were signs that the isolation of the Russian revolution was encouraging a new form of fatalism.

A philosophy of action

Lukács fought to re-establish the active, interventionist core of Marxism against the constant threat that it would degenerate into a sterile science, a process of reading off human history from impersonal, 'objective' developments.

His first step was to insist on the totality of the revolutionary process. Against standard interpretations of Marxism he argued that 'it is not the primacy of economic motives in historical explanation that constitutes the decisive difference between Marxism and bourgeois thought, but the point of view of totality.'[1]

The idea of totality matters because it is only possible to understand the true significance of an event or phenomenon if it is grasped as part of the sum total of processes that make up the capitalist system. The notion of totality is also crucial to understanding the role of consciousness in history.

Consciousness is not something that stands outside history observing, it is itself a part of the process of history, both shaping and being shaped by it. A correct theoretical understanding on the part of the working class is neither an optional extra, nor an inevitable product of the working out of the contradictions of capitalism. It is an absolute necessity if we are to avert disaster, and as Lukács argued, it becomes more important rather than less so in a revolutionary crisis.

> *As the decisive battle in the class struggle approaches, the power of a true or false theory to accelerate or retard progress grows in proportion. The 'realm of freedom', the end of the 'pre-history of mankind' means precisely that the power of the objectified, reified relations between men begins to revert to man. The closer this process comes to its goal the more urgent it becomes for the proletariat to understand its own historical mission and the more vigorously and directly proletarian class consciousness will determine each of its actions.* [HCC 69-70]

From where does this consciousness come? For Lukács, as for Marx, socialism is not a blueprint but a result of the fight of working people for their interests. It is both a product of capitalism and the negation of capitalism. But if socialism is in the interests of the working class, the question becomes, why aren't the majority of workers permanently fighting for it? In fact, how come we haven't got there already?

Lukács' answers revolved around two ideas. First, he argued that workers are in a unique position from which to understand the way the capitalist system works. At the same time, he saw that life under capitalism creates a sense of powerlessness, a separation between the individual and historical process. It is this double reality that explains the mixed, contradictory consciousness that most people exhibit most of the time.

Lukács' three key works of the 1920s still form the most systematic theoretical account of how this contradictory consciousness is created and how it can be overcome. They are partly reflections on the lessons of his own experience. They were also products of his re-examination of the philosophical basis of Marxism, which was triggered by his first systematic reading of Lenin. *History and Class Consciousness* and his other books from the period were first denounced and then suppressed by the Stalinists. They promoted too active, too subversive a version of Marxism for the new bureaucratic rulers. Indeed Lukács himself disowned them at the end of the 1920s. But *History and Class Consciousness* has proved irrepressible. Until its reprint in 1967 it had an underground existence, reappearing in pirated form whenever insurgent struggle re-emerged.

As Stalin's regime strangled the revolution in Russia and misdirected revolutionaries around the world, Lukács moved away from revolutionary politics and dedicated himself to literary criticism. His hopes for revolutionary change rose once again towards the end of his life, in the late 1960s. But what follows is neither a biography of Georg Lukács nor a description of how his ideas evolved and changed during his long life. Others have done that job brilliantly. The aim here is to introduce the work of Lukacs' revolutionary years to people who are once again struggling to change the world.

2. Ideology, class and crisis

After speaking at a discussion circle, Lukács was once asked, *"Isn't there a deep bond between the factory owner and the worker?"* He replied, *"Yes quite decidedly. The same as that between the spider and the fly in its web."* [2]

People are often surprised at how much time Lukács spends in *History and Class Consciousness* on the ideas and attitudes of the ruling class. The reason is that ruling class ideas are uniquely powerful in capitalist society, because of the unprecedented domination of a single economic system and the interdependence of the two main classes.

But the domination of ruling class ideas is not complete. Capitalism is a system based on contradictions, and the fragmented experience of immediate reality under capitalism normally conceals the totality of relations that make up the system. The various mediations at work within capitalism – the law, education, political institutions – contain the fundamental contradictions most of the time. They cannot, however, resolve them, and this fact finds expression in bourgeois thought.

The ideas of the ruling class

Bourgeois thought is inconsistent. This inconsistency is suggested historically by the fact that, precisely at the time that the bourgeoisie had achieved their great victory over the feudal order, they were faced with a new enemy: the working class. The freedom which had been the bourgeoisie's rallying cry during their great revolutionary struggles had to be replaced or accompanied by new forms of repression. The bourgeoisie had to write class struggle out of history even though it had itself been created by class struggle. The result is that in suppressing the notion of collective human struggle, the ruling class is left clinging to a belief in the power of the individual and at the same time in that of inhuman forces.

Inconsistency is structured into bourgeois thought by the nature of capitalism. First, the capitalists are more interested in the expansion of capital than production itself. So although the central questions of society are questions of production – who produces what, how and for whom – these are secondary for the capitalist, who just wants to produce and sell commodities. Capitalism may foreground the individual and individual freedom of choice as its central motivating idea but the economic structures which it has created have ruthlessly destroyed the conditions for individuality.

Second, although capitalism is a social force, it is a blind one. Because capitalists compete with one another, the overall function and social impact of the system takes place 'unbeknown to them, and, as it were, against their will and behind their backs' [HCC 63].

So, although capitalists act as a class in pushing society forward, they experience this process as something independent of them. It is a process they therefore cannot fully understand.

Capitalists are, for example, in denial about the systemic nature of economic crises. Almost every boom is accompanied by claims that the cycle of boom and bust is ended. To recognise that crises are structured into the way the system works would be to recognise the irrational, destructive nature of the capitalist system as a whole. As Marx commented, each new financial crisis 'heaps theoretical fright on top of practical panic,' at which time the capitalists 'shudder before the impenetrable mystery in which their own economic relations are shrouded' [HCC 63].

The bourgeoisie then attempts to embrace the whole of society with its values, but it cannot grasp the real relations of the society over which it has so much micro-control.

The tragic dialectics of the bourgeoisie can be seen in the fact that it is not only desirable but essential for it to clarify its own class interests on every particular issue while at the same time such a clear awareness becomes fatal when it is extended to the question of the totality. [HCC 65]

Lukács explains how the capitalist class has historically responded to this situation by trying to find formal, false totalities to hide or explain away the real foundations of bourgeois society. In the nineteenth century they flirted with mystical concepts about the 'essence' of history and the state. Property, freedom and unrestricted initiative were regarded as sacred.

The temptation of mysticism is in constant tension with the need for rationality to serve the needs of production. The move to various forms of capitalist planning in the twentieth century partially eroded the basis for openly mystical explanations of how the world was working, at least in the capitalist mainstream.

But the opposition between abstract, formal laws and a fragmented, atomised, immediate reality is still with us. Everything from academic research to the daily news is parcelled into specialised, separate categories. This leads to a loss of a sense of how things are connected and therefore the nature of their real significance. Events or facts are isolated from any history or explanation, which in turn encourages an acceptance of reality as given and unchangeable.

Meanwhile, mystifying universals have been making a comeback since the 'victory' of the free market. Since the failure of Keynesian economics at the end of the 1970s and up to the current economic crisis, the market was once more treated as a benign force of nature. Francis Fukuyama's 'end of history' was a strange case of a negative universal, a wished-for reversion to a spontaneous, natural order, which the Western powers perversely tried to impose on various parts of the world by force.

The language of human rights appears to be a more positive universal framework. But while benign enough as ideas, these rights remain unobtainable abstractions for the majority of the world's population. And as abstract principles, they contain no clue as to how to change the facts on the ground.

Lukács' description of the bourgeois understanding of the world retains its relevance: '...reality disintegrates into a multitude of irrational facts and over these a network of purely formal 'laws' emptied of content is then cast' [HCC 155].

Crisis and consciousness

The inconsistency in the capitalists' worldview periodically becomes a liability. Although capitalism 'has created a form for the state and a system of law corresponding to its needs and harmonising with its own structure,' [HCC 95] Lukács points out the limits of this process.

Ultimately, the formal structure of laws cannot suppress the irrationality of the system. Investment decisions are driven by the needs of profit, which are not the same as social needs, and so 'theory and practice are brought into irreconcilable opposition to each other' [HCC 64].

So, for example, 'non-economic' capitalist institutions can't simply mirror the irrationalities of the economic system or they would be unable to function. The legal system or the political world have to have some internal coherence and therefore relative autonomy from the economic base. But the inescapable domination of the economic process means that contradictions cannot be avoided. It leads to the embarrassment of a justice system that claims all are equal before the law, but will only allow access to court for the rich. It creates a political system that claims to be based on one person one vote but allows corporate lobbyists special access to its representatives.

The ruling class tries to conceal or resolve these

inconsistencies by re-enforcing the separation of the political, legal, economic realms and so on. But this fiction starts to break down at times of crisis. Crises show the accidental and chaotic relation of two sides of what is normally presented as a seamless economic whole. Meanwhile, in the midst of panic, the role of state institutions is exposed, as politicians vote to bail out the banks, or police forces attack unemployed protestors. Crises don't automatically create an anti-capitalist consciousness, but they open up the possibility for its development.

> *In periods of economic crisis the position is quite different. The unity of the economic process now moves within reach. So much so that even capitalist theory cannot remain wholly untouched by it, though it can never fully adjust to it. ...Even if the particular symptoms of crisis appear separately (according to country, branch of industry, in the form of 'economic' or 'political' crisis, etc.), and even if in consequence the reflex of the crisis is fragmented in the immediate psychological consciousness of the workers, it is still possible and necessary to advance beyond this consciousness. And this is instinctively felt to be a necessity by larger and larger sections of the proletariat.* [HCC 75]

Working class ideas

Lukács starts from the similarities of capitalist experience for worker and capitalist. But these similarities are partial and can break down.

The bourgeois can live with the contradiction, on the one hand, of thinking that reality emanates from his own actions, and on the other worshiping the forces of the market. It may result in an incoherent view of the world, but at least it is one that fits his class interests.

The experience of the worker is different. The worker

experiences the reality of capitalism as a given, an external unchanging reality; the illusion of having any influence over events is much less powerful than for the boss:

> *In every aspect of daily life in which the individual worker imagines himself to be the subject of his own life he finds this to be an illusion that is destroyed by the immediacy of his existence... And by selling this, his only commodity, he integrates it (and himself: for his commodity is inseparable from his physical existence) into a specialised process that has been rationalised and mechanised, a process that he discovers already existing, complete and able to function without him and in which he is no more than a cipher reduced to an abstract quantity, a mechanised and rationalised tool.* [HCC 165-66]

What is more, the fundamental relations of capitalism periodically erupt into open conflict, breaking through the fiction of universal laws. Because it is driven by competition, the process of commodification means that the capitalist is constantly increasing his quantitative take from the worker – trying to keep wages down, trying to shorten holidays or even lunch breaks – compared to the next capitalist. Workers will naturally do their best to resist this, and this resistance can create quantitative limits to accumulation.

But it is in the struggle over labour time, and the reward for labour, that commodification itself can find a limit in the consciousness of conflicting interest. When workers fight for better conditions, better pay or shorter hours, the basic antagonism between bosses and workers starts to become clear.

> *The instant that this consciousness arises and goes beyond what is immediately given we find in concentrated form the basic issue of class struggle:*

the problem of force. For it is at this point where the 'eternal laws' of capitalist economics fail and become dialectical and are thus compelled to yield up the decisions regarding the fate of history to the conscious actions of men. [HCC 178]

3. The puzzle of class consciousness

Marx made two points about consciousness under capitalism that can appear to contradict each other. On the one hand, he said 'the ideas of the ruling class are in every epoch the ruling ideas,'[3] and on the other hand, that socialism is the emancipation of the working class 'must be the work of the working class.'[4] This begs the question, if capitalist ideas are so dominant, where can the ideas and impetus for liberation come from? Lukács, more clearly than anyone, explained this paradox and how it can be overcome in practice.

Most radical explanations of why people put up with capitalism focus on ideas. As Marx argued, the media, schools, universities, all are controlled by the ruling class. While debate is allowed within certain limits, criticism of the system as a whole is considered exotic.

There is a symbiotic relationship between the media and mainstream politics. Social democratic leaders justify moderating their demands by citing the power of the media, but their parties have long encouraged people to believe that the only way to change society is piecemeal, through the electoral process. They accept the capitalist framework and by accepting it, encourage 'realistic' expectations. They promote compromise with, and nowadays capitulation to, pro-business agendas.

Most of the time the leaders of the trade union movements take a sectional and modest view of what is possible through the self-activity of workers. They are wary of encouraging action that challenges the law, or action for political ends. In turn the media take their cue from official politics and 'civil society'.

These political, media and civil society institutions, all part of what Marx called the superstructure of capitalist society, play a vital role in securing consent for the capitalist class. But the obvious problem with a purely propaganda or institutional model of control is that it can help explain passivity but not resistance. Despite the media's hostility and the trade union leaders' hesitancy, strikes do take place; people do fight back against the priorities of the system.

Life under capitalism

In *History and Class Consciousness* Lukács does take the role of capitalist institutions as mediating elements into account. But he explains their capacity to secure workers' consent as a product of the lived experience of capitalism. He also explains how and why that same experience can create opposition.

Lukács' starting point is the fact that capitalism turns everything into a commodity, a product whose main purpose is to generate profit for capitalists. Lukács argued it is no accident that the commodity was also Marx's starting point when he wanted to portray capitalist society in its totality in his major works.

> *The problem of commodities must not be considered in isolation or even regarded as the central problem in economics, but as the central, structural problem of capitalist society in all its aspects. Only in this case can the structure of commodity-relations be made to yield a model of all the objective forms of bourgeois society together with all the subjective forms corresponding to them.* [HCC 83]

Commodity production shapes how we experience and understand the world. It reduces quality to quantity and it conceals the overall process of exploitation in an immediate world of buying and selling. Echoing Marx's words in *Capital*, Lukács described how commodification has the effect of giving relations between people the character of things, of 'reifying' them.

In the process relationships acquire a '"phantom objectivity", an autonomy that seems so strictly rational and all-embracing as to conceal every trace of its fundamental nature' [HCC 83]. This is why commodities have what Marx called 'the character of a fetish'. Like primitive fetishes made by humans and then worshipped as gods, commodities come to rule over us even though we create them ourselves.

We can only grasp the full impact of this process of reification when we realise that the transformation of labour itself into a commodity is the essential condition of a society based on commodification. If the value of goods is going to be determined by the labour time necessary for their production, labour power must be fully integrated into this rational, universally-quantified system. The worker must sell her labour power like any other commodity on the market.

> *Neither objectively nor in his relation to his work does man appear as the authentic master of the process; on the contrary, he is a mechanical part incorporated into a mechanical system. He finds it already pre-existing and self-sufficient, it functions independently of him and he has to conform to its laws whether he likes it or not.* [HCC 89]

Commodification shapes the physical process of work itself and our understanding of it. Work becomes dominated by rationalisation, a high division of labour, repetition and obsession with quantity rather than quality. The finished article no longer appears as the object of a process at all. The fragmented process of production of the object ends up producing a fragmented subject: 'The personality can do no more than look on helplessly while its own existence is reduced to an isolated particle fed into an alien system' [HCC 90].

Reification then has three reinforcing effects on consciousness. It hides the real, human relations of capitalism; it makes the system appear as if it is driven by an inhuman, preordained logic; and it makes workers feel powerless to do anything about it.

It is often pointed out that Lukács, through his reading of *Capital*, arrived at a concept almost identical with the idea of alienation contained in Marx's *Economic and Philosophical Manuscripts*, which was written in 1844 but not published until 1932.

But he did more than that. He broke new ground by showing how reification permeated the whole of capitalist society and laid the foundations for the first 'unified structure of consciousness' in history. He went on to explore the implications of this for radical politics.

Lukács argued that the state of mind generated by the experience of work at the sharp end of capitalist production is suffused throughout the institutions of capitalist society.

> *The atomisation of the individual is, then, only the reflex in consciousness of the fact that the 'natural laws' of capitalist production have been extended to cover every manifestation of life in society; that – for the first time in history – the whole of society is subjected, or tends to be subjected, to a unified economic process, and that the fate of every member of society is determined by unified laws.* [HCC 91-92]

Lukács argued for example that bureaucracies are a corollary to the factory system:

> *Bureaucracy implies the adjustment of one's way of life, mode of work and hence of consciousness, to the general socio-economic premises of the capitalist*

economy, similar to that which we have observed in the case of the worker in particular business concerns. The formal standardisation of justice, the state, the civil service etc., signifies objectively and factually a comparable reduction of all social functions to their elements, a comparable search for the rational formal laws of these carefully segregated partial systems. [HCC 98]

So way beyond the profit-making workplace, in institutions across society, tasks are reduced to quantifiable functions, to 'unit throughput', in processes that acquire autonomy from the personality and therefore from human judgement. Even for those dealing directly with other human beings, the sense of overall purpose is lost, all sense of cause and effect obscured.

Lukács gives the example of the journalist whose powers of empathy, judgement, knowledge and expression are divorced from personality, and who is placed in an unnatural isolation when confronting the facts or events he or she 'reports' on. 'The journalist's "lack of convictions", the prostitution of experiences and beliefs is comprehensible only as the apogee of capitalist reification' [HCC 100].

The fatal flaw

So far this all sounds like good news for the capitalist; on closer inspection, problems appear. Most important of these is the fact that the commodification of the world has limits. The most serious limitation is discovered in the very process of commodifying labour power. Labour power is in Marx's words 'a peculiar commodity' because its owner, the worker, can try and limit its consumption by the purchaser and even become conscious of its status as a commodity.

Capitalism then has a problem. The very process by which it achieves its profits can also be the process which generates opposition to it. The opposition starts as partial: a sectional struggle over pay, redundancies or closure, which may or may not be successful. But such workers' struggles always have the potential to go further. The very outbreak of a dispute over pay or conditions at work is a demonstration that the logic of commodification, the fragmented rationality of market forces, hides a deeper, more antagonistic process.

Consequently when class struggle erupts on a large scale, it tends to lead to sudden shifts in consciousness. When workers start to become conscious of their position as commodities in society, it can change the way they act and understand the world. Once that step has been taken the fetish character of every commodity can start to become clear, based as it is on the commodity character of labour power.

This means that the necessary penetration of the commodity into almost every aspect of life under capitalism is also a liability. It means that the web of exploitative relations extends way beyond the traditional working class or those in unions. Casualised workers, people who work in state jobs, people in jobs that used to be regarded as professional or middle class, students who experience their colleges as factories and have to do part-time jobs to pay for the privilege of an education, all have personal experience of commodification and can be drawn into resistance to it. The self-consciousness of workers that can arise from struggle is the starting point for an understanding of the totality of society.

> *Now that this core is revealed it becomes possible to recognise the fetish character of every commodity based on the commodity character of labour power: in every case we find its core, the relation between men, entering into the evolution of society.* [HCC 169]

The historical importance of the emergence of the

working class lies most of all in this relationship to reality.

> *Only when a historical situation has arisen in which a class must understand society if it is to assert itself; only when the fact that a class understands itself means that it understands society as a whole, and when, in consequence, the class becomes both the subject and the object of knowledge; in short, only when these conditions are all satisfied will the unity of theory and practice, the precondition of the revolutionary function of the theory, become possible.*
> [HCC 2-3]

The limits of economic struggle

Lukács explained why working class resistance is more or less a permanent part of capitalist reality and how it is the key to the development of a real understanding of how the system works. But he also explained how such resistance and understanding can be contained.

The immediate reality of capitalist life is linked by a series of mediations to the system as a whole. Active resistance is the beginning of the overcoming of these relations. But passive, contemplative attitudes can reassert themselves, even at times of widespread struggle.

Previous revolutionary classes have been able to make revolutions without developing a total critique of the old order. The bourgeoisie had developed an economic base within feudal society and could create an effective revolutionary alliance that left economic inequality intact. But, because of the way capitalism dominates every aspect of society, this is no longer true of workers.

> *As the bourgeoisie has the intellectual, organisational and every other advantage, the superiority of the proletariat must lie exclusively in its ability to see society from the centre, as a coherent*

whole. [HCC 69]

Working class revolution has to be fully conscious or it will not happen.

It was for this reason that Lukács insisted on drawing out both sides of Marx's understanding of workers' consciousness. On the one hand, Marx fought against utopian ideas. For Marx the utopians' problem was that they weren't able to 'give an account of what passes before their eyes and to make of that their mouthpiece.'[5] For the utopian, the new world has to be brought from outside social struggles, from superior consciousness. In Marx's words, for the utopians 'consciousness approaches society from another world and leads it from the false path it has followed back to the right one' [HCC 78]. If it is to be a realistic prospect, change must be rooted in actually existing social processes.

On the other hand, Lukács quotes Marx warning against the idea that struggle automatically leads down the road to socialism. Spontaneous struggle only opens up the *possibility* of increased understanding and confidence.

> *The working class ought not to exaggerate to themselves the ultimate consequences of these everyday struggles. They ought not to forget they are fighting with effects, but not with the causes of those effects; …that they are applying palliatives, not curing the malady. They ought therefore, not to be exclusively absorbed in these unavoidable guerrilla fights… instead of simultaneously trying to change it, instead of using their organised forces as a lever for the final emancipation of the working class, that is to say, the ultimate abolition of the wages system.*[6]

Economic struggles cannot in themselves overthrow reification. In every struggle there is still unevenness in the way consciousness develops, and there is also still a strong tendency to treat economics and politics as separate. Concern for immediate quantitative gain can go hand in hand with vague utopian or ethical idealism. Utopianism had its origins in a period before the working class was fully developed, but as Lukács pointed out, it continues to have a hold because it fits the alienated experience of life under capitalism and the fragmented way the bourgeoisie conceive of the world.

Utopianism can take different forms. One of them is reformism, or revisionism, as Lukács called it: the belief that a better world will be delivered from above, by others. But there is a long history of apparently more radical socialists separating the idea of socialism from day-to-day struggles by retreating into abstract propaganda for socialism.

> *Do not let us forget either that every attempt to rescue the 'ultimate goal' or the 'essence' of the proletariat from every impure contact with – capitalist – existence leads ultimately to the same remoteness from reality, from 'practical, critical activity' and to the same relapse into the utopian dualism of subject and object, of theory and practice to which Revisionism has succumbed. The practical danger of every such dualism shows itself in the loss of any directive for action.* [HCC 22-23]

Such paralysis can only be avoided if the left grasps the unity of theory and practice; understanding that it is precisely the development and application of class consciousness on and in the social process that can overthrow reification.

The final reason why economic struggles in themselves can't lead to fundamental change flows directly from the others. The complex of institutions that protect the capitalist system – parliament, the law, the media, the police – can only be effectively challenged by conscious political strategising. The danger is always that the left falls back into accepting the division between politics and economics, believing that economic struggle will somehow in itself transform the system.

Social democratic parties actively encourage the separation between economics and politics embedded in the structure of capitalism. Accepting such a division takes the working class back into the enemy territory of partial reforms, where the bourgeoisie has huge superiority, through its knowledge, culture, routine and brute ownership. Transforming society requires grasping capitalism as a whole:

> *In the absence of a real understanding of the interaction between politics and economics a war against the whole economic system, to say nothing of its reorganisation, is quite out of the question.* [HCC 78]

The job of socialists is to make the struggle conscious, to find the link between the everyday and the general, not just in theory but in practice.

> *Only when the immediate interests are integrated into a total view and related to the final goal of the process do they become revolutionary, pointing concretely and consciously beyond the confines of capitalist society.* [HCC 71]

4. Do dialectics matter?

Marxists have often taken the view that Marxism has made philosophy redundant. During the period of the Second International, leading Marxists regarded philosophical questions as abstract matters with no bearing on politics. Capitalism was creating the conditions that would create socialism, so understanding how consciousness could play an active role in changing the world was not a priority. Some of the leading socialist theoreticians of the period saw no problem with adopting the positions of bourgeois philosophers when debates did arise.

When Stalinism arose on the defeat of the revolutionary wave of the early 1920s it was accompanied by the freezing of Marxism into the 'science' of dialectical materialism. Once again Marxism was regarded as a way of understanding laws of social development, which operated independently of humans. Ideas were treated as direct products of economic and social development.

In the words of Laszlo Rudas, a member of the emerging Stalinist bureaucracy, in his critique of *History and Class Consciousness*:

> *Today's society is subjected to certain laws, which prescribe the future direction of society just as necessarily as the direction of a stone that has been thrown is prescribed by the laws of gravity. The stone does not know that its fall is prescribed by natural forces, and it might just as well be the case that at this moment the proletariat knows nothing of its role either... since the proletariat consists not of stones but of people, who possess consciousness, so they will become aware of their historical mission in time.*[7]

Such arguments obviously raise more questions than they answer. But they have become the basis for common caricatures of Marxism. This has caused enormous damage. These caricatures reinforce passivity and create easy intellectual targets for enemies of the left. They have also disorientated many serious students of Marxism, who have reacted against their crude determinism by abandoning the concept of determination altogether.

Lukács argued that such fatalism had nothing in common with Marxism or Leninism. Adopting such attitudes leads away from shaping the future towards tail-ending reality, an attitude that Lenin denounced in *What is to be Done*? Marx and Lenin had an entirely different understanding of the relationship between subjective activity and objective conditions.

The rise of such fatalistic ideas was encouraged by particular social and political developments; the stabilisation and expansion of capitalism in the second half of the nineteenth century and the isolation and defeat of the Russian revolution by the late 1920s. But surrender to the passive attitudes that capitalism encourages is a constant danger for the left. A dialectical understanding of reality is key to resisting it.

Marx and the dialectic

Marx's famous quotation, 'philosophers have *interpreted* the world, in various ways; the point is to *change* it'[8] is often assumed to indicate hostility to all philosophy. In fact it comes from a series of propositions that Marx wrote while developing his own theory of knowledge. It is, rather, part of an attack on passive, contemplative philosophy.

Mainstream bourgeois philosophy had found no way to bridge the gulf between thought and being, between what goes on in our minds and external reality. Overcoming this division was a crucial step for Marx in developing a theory of human liberation.

Before Marx two trends dominated philosophy. The

materialists recognised that a world existed external to human sensation and thought, but grappled with the problem of how we can understand this world when it can only be perceived through the impressions it makes on our senses. A simple correspondence theory of the mind worked up to a point, but the idea that our brains faithfully reflected reality became redundant as soon as there was any controversy about the nature of that reality.

When questions emerged, some philosophers like John Locke tried to make a distinction between 'correct' and 'incorrect' impressions of the world. The problem was finding criteria with which to make that judgement. Others like David Hume ultimately drew the conclusion that we could know nothing with certainty and that truth was nothing more than a projection of our own minds.

The second strand were idealists. They believed that the key to truth lay in human reasoning. To be true, an idea had to be deducible from basic principles. It was not that they believed reality didn't exist; it was more that they privileged reality produced by human beings, or they believed the world to be made in our image.

Neither approach was able to overcome the conceptual split between human consciousness on the one hand and an intractable, independent reality on the other. The greatness of the bourgeois philosopher Immanuel Kant was precisely his open recognition of the fact that philosophy had failed to reconcile these two sides of reality. For Kant, in his *Critique of Pure Reason*, these two poles became frozen into an unalterable foundation of human existence.

The greatness of Hegel was that he took the first steps towards creating a philosophical system that could overcome the separation between thought and reality. Hegel understood reality as a historical process that changed through time. But he also saw reality as a totality, of which consciousness was a part. History was the working out in the human mind of the rational laws that underpin the world. It was the notion of an internally contradictory totality in a constant process of change that was the core of what Hegel called dialectics.

Marx and Engels regarded this as his decisive breakthrough and they adopted the dialectical method. However they reversed its terms. For Hegel the dialectic was the working out through history of the Absolute Spirit, eventually coming to consciousness in the minds of philosophers. For Marx, consciousness was both a product of social being and an active element within it:

> *Already with Hegel, the absolute spirit of history has its material in the masses, but only finds adequate expression in philosophy. But the philosopher appears merely as the instrument by which the absolute spirit, which makes history, arrives at self-consciousness after the historical movement has been completed. The philosopher's role in history is thus limited to this subsequent consciousness, for the real movement is executed unconsciously by the absolute spirit. Thus the philosopher arrives post festum.* [HCC 16]

Marx's great philosophical innovation was to put real living human beings at the heart of the dialectic, and so move the problem of the relation between being and consciousness from the realm of ideas to the real world.

Knowledge itself then becomes a practical active question:

> *The question whether objective truth can be attributed to human thinking is not a question of theory but is a practical question. Man must prove the truth, i.e. the reality and power, the this-sidedness of his thinking in practice. The dispute over the reality or non-reality of thinking that is isolated from practice is a purely scholastic question.*[9]

Knowledge under capitalism

For Marx then, it is through activity that thought and being are linked in reality. It is by interacting with the natural and the social worlds that we gain understanding. However, this does not mean achieving knowledge is unproblematic. Thought and being are part of a unity, but they are not identical. If they were then we wouldn't need any theory. As Marx pointed out, all science 'would be superfluous if the outward appearance of things coincided with their essence' [HCC 8].

Lukács argued that it is only with the development of capitalist society that the possibility of a genuine consciousness of reality emerged.

> In feudal society man could not yet see himself as a social being because his social relations were still mainly natural. Society was far too unorganised and had far too little control over the totality of relations between men for it to appear to consciousness as the reality of man... It was necessary for the proletariat to be born for social reality to become fully conscious. The reason for this is that the discovery of the class-outlook of the proletariat provided a vantage-point from which to survey the whole of society... because for the proletariat total knowledge of its class situation is a vital necessity, a matter of life and death; because its class situation becomes comprehensible only if the whole of society can be understood. [HCC 19-20]

But even under capitalism the experience of reality, including active interaction with it, doesn't provide us with immediate, direct access to the totality of social relations.

This is because no simple activity overcomes the fragmentation of life in our commodified world. Lukács took on at length the view of some of his critics that the process of work, or the position of workers in society, guaranteed enlightenment. Such a view ignored the fact that the labour process is fragmented and mystified under capitalism. The idea that workers' class position spontaneously produces an understanding of the world would belie the need for any ideological struggle at all.

> *Of course revolutionary practice grows on the basis of a social being that motivates this activity. But not elementally, not spontaneously, rather precisely through the workers becoming conscious of the social, historical preconditions of their activity, the objective tendencies of economic development, which have motivated their activity and which push beyond these forms of social being, become conscious and extend this consciousness.* [TD 129]

In *Tailism and the Dialectic*, Lukács goes on to argue that scientific experiment also provides no guarantee of comprehending reality. Although experiments provide important data that are vital to solving particular problems, they provide only a fragmentary glimpse of the real, a glimpse which is torn out of the process of which it is a part. Experimentation tends to assume a position of neutral observation and therefore is blind to the human, social context of the experiment.

Despite the common caricatures of Marxism, it is precisely not a theory in which thought is entirely dependent on a pre-existing, separate 'being'. Thought and being are part of a totality, but a differentiated, dialectical totality. If thought and being were identical, we would be back to the notion of an automatic, predetermined history. The working class is the object of history; it can only fulfil its potential of becoming the subject of history through a theoretical understanding of its own activity.

'Correct' class consciousness
We have seen that Lukács stresses how it is the radical activity of fighting for our class interests that opens up the

possibility of grasping the totality of society. In the process of strikes or other struggles, people make all sorts of connections, but even here the dialectic between thought and reality doesn't come to an end. Struggle creates big leaps in consciousness, it very often helps to break down any racist or sexist attitudes in a workforce, for example, and it almost always sharpens people's sense of the class bias of the media. But partial struggles don't automatically lead to an understanding of the total structure of society.

The revolutionary significance of such partial experiences will only become clear on a broad enough scale if they are illuminated by a wider overview of the context; that is, if they are located in the totality of relations. This is what Lukács meant when he asserted in *Tailism and the Dialectic* the primacy of 'higher' theoretical categories in Marxism:

> *There must be clarity about the fact that the so-called simple categories are not trans-historical elements of the system, but are just as much products of historical developments as the concrete totalities to which they belong, and that, therefore, simple categories are correctly grasped from higher, more complicated, more concrete ones.* [TD 112]

An understanding of the totality of capitalist relations needs to be brought to bear on the partial experiences of the movement if they are to be understood and if the movement is to go forward.

The question then arises: if an understanding of the capitalist totality doesn't come directly from working class experience, even experience of struggle, where can it come from? Where is the vantage point from which we can gain a real picture of the contours of capitalism, of the totality of the system?

Lukács has regularly been criticised for his notion of a 'correct' or 'imputed' class consciousness, as opposed to the ideas that particular workers may have in their heads at any particular time. In the 1920s Laszlo Rudas attacked him by sarcastically asking about the 'third place' where Lukács believed consciousness realises itself. Is it, he asked, 'in the head of a God or many gods, perhaps in the head of Madame History or some such thing?' [TD 74]. Ever since, other critics have raised doubts that there can be a point of view from which we can judge the correctness of class consciousness.

To take this position to its logical conclusion would be either to capitulate completely to given reality or collapse once again into idealism, either giving up trying to change the world, or trying to change it according to abstract and arbitrary principles. No effective activist can really operate on the basis that there is no correct way to understand reality.

In reply to Rudas, Lukács argued that in reality the idea of correct class consciousness informs the practice of all agitators or organisers. Any such activist 'would ask Comrade Rudas whether he had the right to dispute the proletarian class consciousness of a strike-breaker, indeed even a wavering worker' [TD 72].

Other critics, including Louis Althusser, have in fact taken Lukács to task for seeing Marxism as being too direct an expression of working class practice. As Michael Löwy points out, these criticisms may fairly be said to cancel each other out.[10]

In defending imputed or ascribed class consciousness, Lukács is not arguing that revolutionary consciousness has to come from outside the experience of struggle.[11] There is, of course, no static or ahistorical point of view from which society can be effectively comprehended.

Lukács' understanding of genuine class consciousness can only be understood through the idea of a dialectical interaction between activity and theory over time. The key to correct class consciousness, and an effective understanding of the world, lies, in Marx's words, 'in human practice and in the comprehension of this practice.'[12]

Real historical struggles, from the Paris Commune to the explosions of struggle around the world in the 1960s and 1970s have shown that working people have an interest in challenging the priorities of capitalism and trying to develop alternatives. These struggles have inspired the most comprehensive and coherent attempts to explain how capitalism works, which have then been re-tested in practice.

Socialist theory is nothing other than the condensed understanding of the history of class struggle. Revolutionary consciousness can only be developed through a constant dialectical interaction between the lived experience of struggle and this hard-won theoretical understanding. It must involve not only using theory to guide practice but reassessing theory in the light of new experiences. One of the reasons there is so much resistance to dialectics is that holding this dynamic interaction of practice and theory in motion raises the question of independent, working class organisation.

5. Spontaneity and organisation

The point of Lukács' analysis of consciousness under capitalism was to lay the groundwork for a theory of revolutionary action. *History and Class Consciousness* ends with two densely-argued essays on organisation. The arguments in Lukács' short 1924 book on Lenin flow directly from the main propositions in *History and Class Consciousness*.

Lukács wrote these works in the aftermath of one of the great breaks in the history of the socialist movement. The Russian revolution of 1917 had involved the Russian revolutionaries splitting with the Second International and breaking with its politics. Around the world, the most militant activists followed the Bolsheviks' lead and set up Communist parties.

The interpretation of the Russian experience internationally was no simple matter. On the one hand, the extent to which socialists in different countries were prepared to break with the methods of the Second International varied. On the other, some activists veered towards a rejection of politics, a revolutionary purism and impatience that was often combined with a belief in workers' spontaneous ability to grasp the need for revolution. Sometimes the two mistakes – underestimating the importance of a clear break with reformists and relying on spontaneous revolutionary consciousness – were combined.

Lukács' own experience in Hungary was a case in point. The Hungarian Communist Party leadership, including Lukács himself, had overestimated the revolutionary consciousness of the working class and underestimated the reformist SDP's inclination to compromise. These mistakes helped ensure the isolation of the revolutionaries and the crushing of the Hungarian Soviet Republic.

Lukács stayed secretly in Hungary for a few months to try and salvage something from the wreckage of the Communist Party, but conditions made this impossible. He only just escaped the country alive. On his return to Vienna in 1919, he began a serious study of the theoretical debates that had informed the Russian revolution and particularly the work of Lenin. It was during the next two years of study and participation in the debates of the Communist International that Lukács completed *History and Class Consciousness.*

More than any other contemporary, Lukács synthesised the experience of these revolutionary years and produced a theoretical explanation of the policies of the Bolsheviks. This involved a critique of the opportunism of the Second International but also an explanation of why reliance on the spontaneous instincts of workers is not an adequate response to betrayal by the reformists.

Organisation before the Bolsheviks

Until the Russian revolution, Marxists had not paid much attention to the theoretical questions of organisation. Marx himself had discussed the definition of communism in principle, criticised the conservatism of the trade unions, helped organise two international federations and celebrated the revolutionary organisations thrown up by the Paris Commune in 1871. But he had never seen national movements of workers' insurrection and so couldn't have predicted how different tendencies in the movement would struggle for influence.

As Lukács pointed out, the great socialist organisations of the Second International developed towards the end of the nineteenth century, when revolutionary action was not on the agenda. Revolution was considered in the abstract but had not become a practical issue, and so questions of revolutionary organisation had not been properly theorised. The result was that organisation was treated as a technical rather than a political matter. Notionally the party was preparing for revolution, but its practice amounted to supporting workers' struggle and standing in elections. In reality it was size that counted in these organisations, and by default the struggle for socialism became the growth of the socialist organisation and the incremental increase in its votes.

Lukács saw such a separation of content and form as a surrender to bourgeois ways of thinking, and one which encouraged compromise with the system. When Social democratic parties supported their respective governments in the First World War, they revealed the extent to which they had internalised capitalist structures of consciousness.

Rosa Luxemburg's challenge

It was the German revolutionary Rosa Luxemburg who first developed a critique of these tendencies, which were most clearly displayed by the German SPD. Her starting point was that the mass actions of workers are the key to change. Mass action was needed to overthrow the system, but also it was also mass struggle that brought people into the movement in the first place. Luxemburg had experienced the way that bureaucratised organisation can dismiss or stand in the way of such initiative in the SPD:

> *The overestimation of or misapprehensions about the role of organisation in the class struggle of the proletariat are usually accompanied by feelings of contempt for the unorganised proletarian masses and for their political immaturity.* [HCC 298]

She had a different view of the role of the party; it lay 'not in the technicalities of the preparations for the mass strike and in supplying its leadership but first and foremost in the political leadership of the whole movement' [HCC 298]. Her rejection of merely technical organisation, her stress on wider political leadership and emphasis on rank and file initiative amounted to a breakthrough for socialist theory.

Luxemburg highlighted the role of self-activity in the liberation of working people more effectively than anyone before her and she had a great influence on Lukács. He called her 'the unsurpassed prophet, the unforgettable teacher and leader of revolutionary Marxism' [HCC 277]. Even as he challenged some of her arguments, he pointed out that towards the end of her tragically short life she moved close to the position of the Bolshevik party by founding the Spartacist League, the forerunner of the German Communist Party.

But Lukács challenged some of her earlier arguments. He believed she put too much weight on spontaneous forms of struggle. He pointed out that in correctly championing the initiative of workers' Luxemburg tended towards an organic concept of change. It was precisely an organic understanding of social transformation that she criticised in the right wing of the SPD. He quotes her, for example, saying:

> The socialist system of society should only be and can only be a historical product, born of the school of its own experiences; and – just like organic nature of which, in the last analysis, it forms a part – it has the fine habit of always producing, along with any real social need, the means to its satisfaction, along with the task simultaneously the solution. [HCC 278]

This idea of an organic ideological growth into socialism not only underestimated the obstacles to full socialist consciousness but could easily lead to strategic error. Luxemburg criticised the Bolsheviks, for example, for counterposing one form of democracy with another by closing down the bourgeois Constituent Assembly in Russia in 1918 and insisting on complete power for the workers councils. She claimed Lenin and Trotsky were being 'rigid and schematic' for believing that such apparently formal questions are important:

> *Yet how all historical experience contradicts this! Experience demonstrates quite the contrary: namely that the living fluid of the popular mood continuously flows around the representative bodies, penetrates them, guides them.* [HCC 279]

Here Luxemburg underestimates the qualitative break involved in workers' revolution. As Lukács had previously pointed out, bourgeois revolutions could appear spontaneous because spreading capitalist relations had already partly undermined feudal society.

If working people need to play a consciously directing role in their liberation, then they need new institutions that allow active, mass participation in politics, not just the casting of ballot papers every so often. A workers' revolution needs radically new forms of organisation because it is aiming to smash the tyranny of unplanned economics. Bourgeois parliaments institutionalise the separation of economics and politics that allow capitalists the freedom to pursue their profits unchallenged.

Ideas and organisation

By relying on spontaneity to overcome conservatism, Lukács argued that Rosa Luxemburg was failing to draw organisational conclusions from her own insights. Before her final break with the SPD, Luxemburg argued that the fight against opportunism should be conducted as an intellectual one within the SPD. The task was to convince the opportunists of their mistakes and so win a majority within a wider socialist organisation.

The problem with this approach is that if the battle

against the opportunists is not allowed to crystallise out into tendencies, it will descend into a series of individual skirmishes in which today's allies can become tomorrow's opponents and no one is any the clearer. Luxemburg had warned of the conservatism created by bureaucracies, but it is precisely this kind of divided organisation that is most vulnerable to bureaucratic control.

Lukács argued that ideas need to be organised to have impact. Reification penetrates deep into capitalist society, workers are brought up within the forms of life of the bourgeoisie and these are not broken in a single stroke. Neither socialist propaganda nor the experience of struggle are in themselves enough to break capitalist domination. Even after major struggles workers can be persuaded to return to 'normality' and to conventional forms of politics. Explicitly revolutionary organisation is necessary to develop a different kind of genuinely liberating politics.

Economic and political crisis provide the conditions in which bourgeois life forms can best be exposed, but even conditions of crisis do not in themselves automatically break them.

> *This ideological transformation does indeed owe its existence to the economic crisis which created the opportunity to seize power. The course it actually takes does not, however, run parallel in any automatic and 'necessary' way with that taken by the crisis itself. This crisis can be resolved only by the free action of the proletariat.* [HCC 311]

6. On Leninism

Lukács' short book on Lenin was a practical condensation of his theoretical work. Written on Lenin's death in 1924, it has sometimes been criticised for idealising Lenin. But the book is really an attempt to formulate the principles behind the methods of the Russian revolutionaries and defend them against gathering enemies. In the process, it demolishes two common caricatures of Lenin and Leninism. First, the idea that Lenin was a ruthless pragmatist, opportunistically twisting and turning to seize and then retain power. Second, the (opposite) stereotype that Lenin imposed rigid dogmas on a reluctant population.

For Lukács, Lenin's essential achievement was to understand the necessity and the special nature of revolutionary organisation and to act on it. Lukács explains why Lenin was convinced of the need for separate revolutionary organisation and shows how this reasoning led to a very particular vision of organisation.

The first reason for independent, revolutionary organisation is the uneven consciousness that exists at all times within the working class. Lenin explained this unevenness by reference to the different economic strata amongst workers, and particularly the development of a privileged 'labour aristocracy'. The explanatory power of this concept has been questioned in light of the central role that has often been played by skilled workers in revolutions. Lukács himself was unsure about the idea.[13]

But the idea of uneven consciousness doesn't need the support of a theory of a labour aristocracy. As we have seen, Lukács' explanation of uneven consciousness flows from the way capitalism atomises people, mystifies relations and produces different, sectional experiences. Even major struggles at least partly reflect this sectionalism. This in itself makes the 'organisational independence of the fully conscious elements of the proletariat indispensable.'[14]

But Lenin's theory of organisation also flowed from a grasp of the complexity of revolutionary process. In the real world revolution is not a standoff between two classes but a tumultuous process that engulfs the whole of society. Any crisis profound enough to open up the possibility of social transformation throws all classes into turmoil and sets up dramatic cross currents in society. As Lenin himself argued, 'whoever expects a "pure" social revolution will *never* live to see one. Such a person pays lip-service to revolution without understanding what revolution is' [LS 48].

Dedicated organisation is necessary to chart a course through this maelstrom, not just to overcome unevenness among workers but to win over other sections of society. The working class is the main agent of change, but to succeed it will need to enlist the support of social groups who are disaffected, yet on their own can't find a solution for society as a whole. This will involve creating a series of alliances with wider social forces and careful selection of demands to take advantage of the fissures that crisis opens up.

> If the proletariat wants to win this struggle, it must encourage and support every tendency which contributes to the break-up of bourgeois society, and do its utmost to enlist every upsurge – no matter how instinctive or confused – into the revolutionary process as a whole. [LS 29-30]

In the process it is necessary to ensure that the working class maintains its leadership role and doesn't subordinate itself to any other group and fall back into a secondary, passive role.

Lenin also judged every situation in its international

context. Internationalism was not an afterthought but a crucial dimension to his judgements. The history of the Russian revolution makes no sense without an understanding of how the Bolsheviks viewed their situation globally. Lenin and Trotsky emphasised from the start that a socialist revolution in Russia could not be successful if it didn't spread. The need to link the global and the local underlines the need for our own mediating structures: our own revolutionary organisation.

It was in fact Lenin's analysis of imperialism that led him to the conclusion that a revolutionary situation was developing. On the one hand, the push to war between the great powers was creating crisis in the core countries. On the other hand, the spread of capitalist development around the world and the imperialist designs of the great powers were creating national movements in hitherto 'unhistoric' nations.

Imperialism had changed the role of national movements. Whereas in the nineteenth century nationalist movements had as their main enemy feudal absolutism, now they were dragged into a world of imperialist rivalry and very often ended up ranged against the great capitalist world powers. Very often such national struggles become objectively revolutionary, at least within the context of an active proletarian revolution.

Lenin always focused on the concrete implications of his analysis. He was clear that the bourgeoisie was no longer capable of completing the tasks of the bourgeois revolutions and of leading a fight against imperialism. At the same time he attacked the idea that this ushered in a period of 'purely proletarian revolution', in which revolution could be reduced to a straight fight to the finish between the workers and the capitalists.

The dangerous practical consequence of this attitude is that all those tendencies towards decay and fermentation which necessarily arise under imperialism (the agrarian, colonial and national questions, etc.), which are objectively revolutionary within the context of the proletarian revolution, are overlooked, or even despised and rebuffed. [LS 48]

In fact the very opposite approach is needed. The bourgeoisie's move towards counter-revolution involves it turning its back on all sorts of groups yet to achieve basic freedoms. In this situation working class politics involves becoming the champion of all these oppressed groups, of pursuing to the end the demands on which the capitalists have reneged. Lukács sums up the argument when he says 'the real revolution is the dialectical transformation of the bourgeois revolution into the proletarian revolution' [LS 48-49].

This way of looking at the political situation in all its mediated complexity demanded dedicated, revolutionary organisation. It also led Lenin towards a distinct type of organisation. Lukács argued that Lenin broke with the old idea that the working class makes the revolution, while the party just gives it general direction. He wrote, 'the old formulation of the question of "making" the revolution is based on an inflexible, undialectical division between historical necessity and the activity of the relevant party' [LS 32].

The party had to do more than make technical preparations for a revolution or confine itself to general education; it also had to try 'to *accelerate* the maturing of these revolutionary tendencies by its actions' [LS 32]. It was an illusion to believe that revolutionary class consciousness could develop without this consistent, active intervention in the struggle over time '*as though the proletariat could gradually evolve ideologically into the revolutionary vocation appropriate to its class*' [LS 24].

Revolutionary organisation was necessary to establish the key link in the chain at any given time, and what were the decisive moments when revolutionaries could make breakthroughs that could transform the situation. In *Tailism and the Dialectic*, Lukács returned to this theme: 'How is it possible even to imagine Lenin's basic idea of the preparation and organisation of revolution without such an active and conscious role of the subjective moment?' [TD 57].

This didn't mean, as is sometimes implied, that that Leninism is simply a theory of isolated moments of opportunity. Subjective and objective factors interact over time. This interaction can lead to the creation of a revolutionary organisation that has the influence and ability to concentrate the subjective factor to such an extent as to transform society. 'The subjective moment reaches in this "moment" its comprehensive significance precisely because and inasmuch as it has already acted consciously and actively during earlier developments' [TD 58].

This conception of socialist organisation as the decisive fusing of the practical and the theoretical involved Lenin in what Lukács called a 'double break with mechanical determinism'. He rejected the Second International idea that the party would inevitably grow and lead the masses to socialism, and argued that such fatalism leads directly to passivity. But he also rejected the 'ideological determinism' behind Luxemburg's ideas – the assumption that capitalism would automatically produce revolutionary consciousness in workers.

And he noted that these two wrong positions, these two different versions of the waiting game, can sometimes be fused together in the same organisation:

> If... it is still held that a spontaneous revolutionary self-education of the masses (through mass action and other experiences), supplemented by theoretically sound party agitation and propaganda, is enough to ensure the necessary development, then the idea of the ideological evolution of the proletariat into its revolutionary vocation cannot truly be said to have

been overcome. [LS 25]

Such an analysis calls for organisation that unites different poles: decisiveness and universality of vision; firmness of principle and tactical flexibility; centralised leadership and the highest level of democracy so that the changing moods and arguments of the movement can be recognised, discussed and acted on.

Socialists need to be involved in the struggle but '*always a step in front*' [LS 35]. Here Lukács doesn't mean simply one step ahead politically or analytically, but rather, theoretical clarity is 'only valuable if it does not stop at a general – merely theoretical – level, but always culminates in the concrete analysis of a concrete situation...' [LS 35]. In other words, socialists must provide concrete leadership while at the same time relating each twist and turn to the wider revolutionary project.

The high degree of tactical flexibility implicit in this model requires discipline. To adjust quickly and decisively, the party must be centralised. 'If the party is not capable of immediately adjusting its interpretation to the ever-changing situation, it lags behind, follows instead of leads, loses contact with the masses and disintegrates' [LS 35].

In order to be able to generalise the best experiences of the movement, it also needs to have a high level of democracy, not just formal democracy but a dynamic interaction between membership and leadership. Leninism is often caricatured as undemocratic and it is sometimes argued that Lukács had a notion of a party separate from the working class that magically embodied correct class consciousness and was therefore 'always right'.

Whatever happened to Lukács after the victory of Stalinism, such a view is utterly wrong about the positions argued in *History and Class Consciousness, Tailism and the Dialectic* and *Lenin: A Study in the Unity of his Thought*. In all these works the stress is on the dynamic relationship between the party – which organises the most advanced workers – and the wider working class. This relationship necessitates internal democracy.

> *The party called upon to lead the proletarian revolution is not born ready-made into its leading role: it, too, is not but is becoming. And the process of fruitful interaction between party and class repeats itself – albeit differently – in the relationship between the party and its members.* [LS 37-38]

In *Tailism and the Dialectic* he discusses the importance of open self-criticism in the party:

> *This development, this raising of the level of class consciousness is, then, not an endless (or finite) progress, not a permanent advance towards a goal fixed for all time, but itself a dialectical process... Precisely, Bolshevik self-criticism with its unprecedented significance for the development of parties and mediated to the whole proletariat through those parties, shows this most clearly.* [TD 78]

Socialist organisation by definition partially separates socialists from the rest of society. But Lukács' stress is time and time again on the importance of socialists also being actively and organically involved in the daily struggles of co-workers and the oppressed, and of the decisive importance of that interaction. Democracy is an essential, irreplaceable component of Lukács' conception of socialist organisation that flows directly from his theory of how consciousness can change under capitalism.

Another criticism of Lukács' explanation of Lenin's organisational concepts is that they discount the impact of reification on socialists themselves. This is a particularly perverse charge to lay against Lukács, who spent so much time dealing with exactly this issue.

In its more extreme form, the argument runs that the

democratic hierarchy in a revolutionary party inevitably leads to a problem of bureaucracy. This is an apolitical approach. Social democratic parties like the Labour Party have limited democracy because their whole policy is to compromise with the system. Reining in the rank and file is therefore a high priority for the leadership.

In trade unions the leaderships often become remote from the rank and file because their aim is not to challenge the status quo in general, but to negotiate with or pressure the bosses and campaign for a better deal for the section of workers they represent. The tendency to compromise is built into trade union leaders' social role, which is why building independent rank and file organisation in the unions is so important.

More fundamentally, to believe in an inevitable bureaucratisation of all organisations under capitalism is to deny that a coherent radicalised subjectivity can ever emerge. The only way to go from there is back to pure spontaneity, and the hope that somehow, without organisation, without theory, people could rise up and overthrow reification of their own accord. As Lukács spent so much time showing, such an approach is itself an acceptance of reification that can only lead to passivity.

The whole point of revolutionary organisation is to overthrow the process of commodification. Its basis is an attack on the contemplative consciousness of the bourgeoisie.

This of course doesn't mean that revolutionaries are immune from the pressures of life under capitalism. To counter the dangers of reification in the party itself, revolutionary organisation has to be built on the dynamic intersection between spontaneous action and theoretical foresight. Lukács argued that one of the things that marks out revolutionary organisation is conscious struggle against passivity in the party itself. Members are required to be much more active than in other political organisations. That is why one of the founding principles of communism in its revolutionary years was that members must be 'involved in constant, day-to-day collaboration' [HCC 316].

Revolutionary organisation exists for a unique purpose: the seizure of control of every aspect of our lives by the great mass of the population. Its whole aim is co-ordinated self-activity and initiative. It rests on the objective possibility that working people can quickly become aware of their class situation in a world torn apart by war and exploitation. And that they have the power to change it.

7. The actuality of revolution?

Lukács' book on Lenin opens with a chapter on what he calls the 'actuality of revolution'. More polite critics try to downplay Lukács' relevance by explaining his ideas as a direct product of a unique revolutionary epoch. They imply that the sense of the actuality of revolution, which for Lukács underlay Lenin's approach, is no longer appropriate.

Such critics misunderstand Lukács and overstate the stability of contemporary capitalism. When Lukács discussed Lenin's belief in the actuality of revolution it is clear he was not referring to the immediate prospects for revolution at a particular moment, but an analysis of a whole historical period. Lenin in fact famously failed to predict the imminence of revolution before February 1917.

His point was that because the bourgeoisie was no longer prepared to carry through its basic democratic mission, the working class could and should now take the leading role in the struggle for democracy and progress, even in countries like Russia, where it remained a small minority. As Lukács said, 'the actuality of revolution means that the bourgeoisie had ceased to be a revolutionary class' [LS 20]. The implication of the bourgeoisie's renunciation of its revolutionary role was that the proletariat now had the possibility of leading humanity through revolutionary action. 'In this sense, as both the objective basis of the whole epoch and the key to an understanding of it, the proletarian revolution constitutes the living core of Marxism' [LS 12].

It was this assessment that forced Lenin to link the

future and the present so concretely, and make Marxism a practical guide to action in a way few had even considered previously. Second International Marxists had openly argued that the revolution could be 'left to the future – to a very distant future' [LS 12] and this inevitably resulted in a passive or routine attitude to immediate questions. Lenin brought his analysis to bear on a daily basis 'to establish firm guidelines for all questions on the daily agenda, whether they were political or economic, involved theory or tactics, agitation or organisation' [LS 13].

How has Lenin's assessment stood the test of time? Lukács himself remarked:

> *Had the historical predictions of the Mensheviks* [moderate socialists] *been correct, had a relatively quiet period of prosperity and of the slow spread of democracy ensued, in which – at least in the backward countries – the feudal vestiges of 'the people' had been swept aside by the 'progressive' classes, the professional revolutionaries would have necessarily remained stranded in sectarianism or become mere propaganda clubs.* [LS 26]

Though the system survived the revolutionary crisis of the early 1920s, the next decade of slump opened up revolutionary possibilities in Spain, France and elsewhere, as Leon Trotsky argued with great urgency.

The Second World War ended with anti-colonial struggles across the world. They resulted in the formation of largely state-run economies in postcolonial countries that with a few exceptions struggled to deliver even the basics for their populations. More recent integration into the world market has produced a few much-promoted 'miracles' in the developing world, but the reality of globalised capitalism is misery for the majority of the world's population.

In the West there was a wave of militant mass strikes

in the US at the end of the Second World War. In Greece, allied forces turned their guns against armed left wing partisans who had liberated large areas of their countries. In Italy in 1945 people were queuing up in the streets to join the Communist Party. In France 600,000 people joined the Communist Party during the war, making it the largest political organisation.

There was, in the words of Marxist historian Gabriel Kolko, a 'revolutionary upheaval simmering below the surface of Europe.'[15] The fact that it never came to the boil can partly be explained by the influence of the Communist parties which had themselves given up on 'the actuality of revolution' and were now actively working against it.

Militant struggle returned to the heart of the system in 1968. The year is best known for insurrectionary riots in US cities, anti Vietnam War protests across the world and images of revolutionary students and workers fraternising in the longest general strike in history in France. But it was followed by five or six years of turbulence around the world, as Italian workers rediscovered their revolutionary traditions, students rioted and workers organised general strikes from Pakistan to Brazil. In Chile, a popular movement for socialism was eventually crushed and a revolution in Portugal threw out a fascist government. In Britain a Labour government came in on the back of the biggest strike wave since the 1920s, promising to 'squeeze the rich until the pips squeak'.

There were moments in these years in France, Italy, Chile, Portugal and elsewhere when revolutionary horizons opened up. As a number of Marxist historians have shown, the fact that these opportunities were not taken must at least partly be put down to the failure of the left to seize its chances.

Since the defeat or decline of these movements in the mid and late 1970s, we have had to live through a period in which the ruling class has had most things going their way. But does that mean socialism is off the agenda? Is it in fact the case that the ruling class has solved the underlying problems that created such bouts of instability throughout the twentieth century?

Thirty years of a neoliberal offensive have inflicted many defeats on the left and the trade union movement, but they have failed to restore rates of profit to boom time levels. Despite the US's initial triumphalism, the collapse of the state-run economies in Russia and Eastern Europe has ushered in a world of increased tension in which US hegemony is under threat. Its response has been a return to imperialist interventions that Lenin and Lukács would have had no problem recognising. Meanwhile, debt crisis, until recently a phenomenon of the periphery, has emerged at the core of the system and threatens to turn recession into slump.

In general it appears as if the mechanisms that stabilised the system during the long post-war boom no longer function. Aggressive corporations dictate policies around the world that threaten the fabric of our lives and the very future of the planet. Continued cross-party support for pro-market policies has led to a crisis of ruling class legitimacy.

The failure of politicians to get to grips with the threat of climate chaos is catastrophic in itself but also symbolic of their inability to deal with the chaos their system creates. Meanwhile, the prospect of these interlocking crises forming a destructive cycle was spelt out by army chiefs on both sides of the Atlantic arguing recently that economic crisis and climate chaos will exacerbate rather than allay imperialist tensions.

The experience of neoliberalism has ensured that workers' struggle has returned in many parts of the world and anti-capitalist and anti-imperialist movements have articulated deep and widespread bitterness. Their slogans and their spirit have revived aspirations for systemic change.

Lukács showed how even in these circumstances

capitalist ways of thinking and living can continue to dominate. Because of the commodification of our world, reformist ideas still have a strong hold even when reformist politicians and parties have abondoned the most minimal reforms.

But the conditions exist for people to take matters into their own hands in a way not seen for more than a generation.

Cynicism with self-serving politicians has coincided with increases in the number of people taking to the streets in protest across the Western world and beyond. Even bourgeois commentators speak of a growing bitterness and alienation in society, and they fear the economic crisis will generate widespread social unrest. But the ruling class is only capable of responding to the crisis by unleashing austerity programmes so fierce they aim to re-engineer our lives completely. Already there have been massive demonstrations, riots and general strikes in the countries most affected by the austerity drives.

Many people are saying this should be the left's moment. And it can be. But only if we organise to seize the opportunity.

Notes

1. Lukács, G. (1971) *History and Class Consciousness*. London: Merlin Press, p. 27. Subsequent references to this work as HCC are given in parentheses after quotations.

2. Levine-Meyer, R. (1973) *Levine: The Life of a Revolutionary*. Farnborough: Saxon House, p. 71.

3. Marx, K. and Engels, F. (1974) *The German Ideology*. London: Lawrence and Wishart, p. 64.

4. Marx, K. (1974) Critique of the Gotha Programme, in *Marx: The First International and After*. London: New Left Review, p. 348.

5. Marx, K. (1995) *The Poverty of Philosophy*, New York: Prometheus Books, p. 136.

6. Marx, K. (1996) *Wage labour and capital and Wages, price and profit*. London: Bookmarks, pp. 119-20.

7. Lukács, G. (2000) *A Defence of History and Class Consciousness: Tailism and the Dialectic*. London: Verso, pp. 66-67. Subsequent references to this work as TD are given in parentheses after quotations.

8. Marx, K. (1975) Theses on Feuerbach, in *Karl Marx: Early Writings*. London: New Left Review, p. 423.

9. Marx, K. (1975) Theses on Feuerbach, in *Karl Marx: Early Writings*. London: New Left Review, p. 422.

10. Löwy, M. (1979) *Georg Lukács – From Romanticism to Bolshevism*. London: NLB, p. 177.

11. After quoting Lenin's famous lines suggesting that correct class consciousness would have to be brought from outside the class – a position Lenin himself revised sometime later – Lukács immediately qualifies the argument. 'However, this is a historical process, and the spontaneous element is the germ seed of a conduct that is conscious of its aims' [TD 82].

12. Marx, K. (1975) Theses on Feuerbach, in *Karl Marx: Early Writings*. London: New Left Review, p. 423.

13. Lukács argued in *History and Class Consciousness* that 'the experiences of the revolutionary struggles have failed to yield any conclusive evidence that the proletariat's revolutionary

fervour and will to fight corresponds in any straightforward manner to the economic level of its various parts' [HCC 305].

14. Lukács, G. (1970) *Lenin: A Study in the Unity of his Thought*, London: NLB, p. 29. Subsequent references to this work as LS are given in parentheses after quotations.
15. Kolko, G. (1990) *The Politics of War: The World and United States Foreign Policy, 1943-1945*. New York: Pantheon Books, p. 429.

Further reading

In addition to the cited works by Lukács and Marx, the following are especially recommended:

Terry Eagleton
Marx and Freedom

Franz Jakubowski
Ideology and Superstructure

Karl Korsch
Marxism and Philosophy

Michael Löwy
Georg Lukács: From Romanticism to Bolshevism

István Mészáros
Lukács' Concept of Dialectic

John Rees
The Algebra of Revolution